All My Mad Mothers

All My Mad Mothers

Jacqueline Saphra

New Jersey Aug '17

To Uncle Lobbums

+ Auntie Joan

All the love + history
is in here. Well,
Some of it anyway!
More to come!

Jacqueline

Nine
Arches
Press

All My Mad Mothers
Jacqueline Saphra

ISBN: 978-1-911027-20-1

First published May 2017 by:

Nine Arches Press
PO Box 6269
Rugby
CV21 9NL
United Kingdom

www.ninearchespress.com

Printed in Britain by:
The Russell Press Ltd.

Nine Arches Press is supported using public funding by the National Lottery through Arts Council England.

Supported using public funding by
**ARTS COUNCIL
ENGLAND**

For my daughters

Contents

IV

I

In the winter of 1962 my mother

gathered up her baby her trembling soul
climbed into the Mini my father had bought
as penance for his bad behaviour drove
until she found herself on Hyde Park Corner
travelling round and round in shrinking circles
not sure how to execute the move outwards
into another lane never having been
properly taught how to make an exit

When I was a child my mother and father lived on different continents. I flew between them. When one was asleep, the other was awake and the telephone rang at all hours. You could never be sure what you heard. Certain phrases were often bent or broken in transit, complete sentences drifted away and were lost in the exchange. Those that arrived intact would generally mutate over time. Airmailed scrawls in permanent ink proved more dependable. Tightly trussed with rubber bands, unable to escape, the words waited immutably in the dark.

My Mother's Bathroom Armoury

Beehive proppers backcomb teasers
Pinpoint pluck of fearful tweezers
Leak of mouthwash morbid flavour
Dutch-cap dusted snap-shut cover
Cutting edge of lady-razor
Glint of sin and lure of danger
Woman's flesh a fading treasure
Braced for pain but honed for pleasure

Caked on flakes of failed concealer
Tell-tale cheeks of blusher-stealer
Crimson smear of lipstick wearer
Smile expander mouth preparer
Burning bleach a making-over
Smudged remains of caked mascara
Iron clamp of eyelash curler
Usual instruments of torture
Bath brimful of scented water
Mother's tricks will pass to daughter

This year   next year   sometime   never

Eddie and the Pessaries

Eddie always carried a supply about his person, she told me – so enlightened for a man in 1953. They would fizz inside her quietly, a novel and acute sensation.

Eddie was her first, my mother said, much better than those later starving artist types: the Antipodean painter who left her for a skinny English master who died of pancreatic cancer; the playwright who, after many wives, developed schizophrenia; the up-and-coming violinist (somewhat younger) who had carpal tunnel and could barely move his wrists.

Every time she had a beer, some Eno's fruit salt or a can of Orangina, she'd feel the fizz and think of Eddie: Eddie, who gave her joy and had a heart and took responsibility (think of the pessaries) but wouldn't do: because as Uncle Leo rightly pointed out, he was a Goy, and Lebanese

although he earned a proper living as a kindly pimp, my mother reminisced, procurer of bi-weekly prostitutes for Uncle Leo who was no sinner, merely a bachelor with Needs. And that was how they met, Eddie and my mother, the night he slipped in through the back door for bit of business with her Uncle Leo while the family was round for Shabbos dinner.

Why did she give up freedom, ballet, photography, figure skating, pottery, fossil hunting, trapeze, playing the piano and French? Imagine, she could have been an archaeologist, a big cheese, a virtuoso or interpreter, not just someone's woman.

But no, she didn't give a toss for these, she wailed: only Eddie, Eddie and his kiss; Eddie, Eddie, Eddie neither artist nor dilettante, her first fizz, her lingering disease.

Sometimes my father fell asleep in his study with a cigarette in his hand and set whole books of love poems on fire. My mother suffered from nerves. My father listened regularly to her heart with his stethoscope until he learned to hate its palpitations. He liked to listen to her brain too. He'd warm the end of the stethoscope in hot water then place it on her temple; tell her to think, think hard.

Sicily

The boys show me their penises, like
Chinese mushrooms but lighter in colour,
and smaller than I expected, limp and silky
in their pleated cowls, so in return, I present
my vagina whose bald pinkness leaves them
unimpressed. The morning's diversion
being over, we wander out on the balcony

to practice spitting, wave at Vespas,
local kids and tourists before we amble
down to lunch where Jane in a kaftan
makes her boys drink milk and strokes
Rudy's freckled arm as he rages again about
Ho Chi Minh and how to get the troops out
till Minnie, prettiest stepmother in the world,

tells a joke about a louse that ends up
in the moustache of a motorcyclist
who's done something to a young lady
wearing a mini skirt and no pants,
Jane laments the lack of a record player
because they brought Sergeant Pepper
which is fucking revolutionary and Rudy

can't get enough of Fixing a Hole.
Jane and Rudy have a word with their boys
about naked bodies on the balcony where
anyone might see, my father quickly says
how Lucy in the Sky with Diamonds
is like tripping without tripping,
and then Minnie is laughing about

the boat, the way my father stopped her
climbing the ladder by pinching
her left nipple between thumb and forefinger
because he knew it made her crazy,
and I decide not to tell my mother how
I dream the flush of Minnie's breasts,
nor offer up the dewy mornings

I'm invited to nestle between bodies,
the strange and spreading heat of skin,
nor talk about those olives stuffed
with pimentos, quick salt licks
of anchovies, cling peaches furred
from the tree, bottles of Chianti breathing,
breathing in their modest little baskets.

My dark-haired mother was a necromancer. She could vanish whole stories by repeating them over and over until they wore out and fell to pieces. This seemed to make her very tired. While she slept, the stories reformed themselves and sidled back into her open mouth. The order was never the same twice.

The Sound of Music

Nobody wanted to be Captain Von Trapp
but we always argued over Gretel.

My sister was the smallest and prettiest.
She couldn't sing in tune

but I didn't dare tell her that,
however much it pained me.

Gretel had only one line:
The Sun has gone to bed and so must I:

whoever was Liesel had to be strong enough
to lift her up and that was always me.

When I heard about the overdose
I could hear nothing but my sister

murdering the melody again,
but fuzzy, like a message

sent across rooftops
through yoghurt pots and string.

Maybe I should have told her.
I didn't understand then

that you can squander a lifetime
trying to stay small and pretty,

believing you have the voice
of an angel if only someone

would hear it and carry you
up the grand staircase to bed.

My Australian stepfather stretched his own canvasses. He had a palette made of hardboard and his ancient brushes shed bristles onto the paintwork. One arm, the painting arm, was shorter than the other. This was because a funnel-web spider had bitten him when he was a baby. They had operated, but were forced to cut some of the bone away. He'd hold his arms out and show me. See? One arm is shorter. That's the painting one.

All My Mad Mothers

My mother gathered every yellow object she could find:
daffodils and gorgeous shawls, little pots of bile
and piles of lemons. Once we caught her with a pair
of fishnet stockings on a stick, trying to catch the sun.

My mother never travelled anywhere without her flippers,
goggles and a snorkel. She'd strip at any opportunity:
The Thames, The Serpentine, the shallows of a garden pond,
a puddle in the park. She was no judge of depth.

My mother was a dipterologist, sucking fruit flies through a straw.
Our house was filled with jars of corpses on display. Sometimes
she'd turn them out, too dead to flee, their wings still glinting,
make them into rainbow chokers, for our party bags.

My mother barely spoke between her bruises:
her low cut gown was tea-stained silk, and from behind
her Guccis or Versaces, she would serve us salty dinners,
stroke a passing cheek, or lay her head on any waiting shoulder.

My mother was an arsonist. She kept a box of matches
in her bra, lined up ranks of candles, ran her pretty fingers
through the flames. At full moon, she would drag
our beds into the garden, set them alight and howl.

My mother was a fine confectioner. We'd come upon her sponges,
softly decomposing under sweaters in a drawer, or oozing
sideways in a filing cabinet. Once, between her pearls
and emerald rings, we found a maggot gateau, iced with mould.

My mother was so hard to grasp: once we found her
in a bath of extra virgin olive oil, her skin well slicked.
She'd stocked the fridge with lard and suet, butter – salted
and unsalted – to ease her way into this world. Or out of it.

II

Crete, 1980

I lived on hard boiled eggs and yoghurt
with a slug or ten of ouzo as my waist grew

waspish and my flesh indifferent
through my lean and solitary season.

I was girlish and abandoned, took my bed
of sand, those oh-so-green and casual boys

for granted, dreamed on beaches
naked, mouth grazed with the taste

of smoke and strangers' kisses,
and I howled into the drunken dark for

stupid reasons and I thought
this was an education.

My first stepmother was blonde and clever. She was on my father's arm when he came to collect me for annual holidays. My two fathers did not dislike each other and sat politely conversing on the sofa; one wielded his stethoscope, the other his paintbrush. It was not entirely clear which of them was in charge.

Getting into Trouble

Mr Giles said he didn't want the school used as a political jousting ground and made me take the pro-abortion poster down, although I explained patiently that the ancient Romans didn't mind it, that the church was okay with it in the 13th Century until quickening (when, they said, the soul enters the body), and the statute books condoned it.

Michelle, who was a Born Again, insisted life was ensouled even before conception; Clare believed that once the foetus was viable it had a right to exist, my mother said she didn't believe in the primacy of the unborn, and I sat in biology wondering if I had a soul, and if I did, where it was. I daydreamed of knitting needles, coat hangers and permanganate.

After my mother came back from hospital – unharmed, grateful and political, only to find that my stepfather had spent her emergency money on canvasses and Carlsberg and dinner with that woman in Portobello Road, she sent me straight to the doctor to get myself a Dutch cap.

My boyfriend, who was stupid but useful, told all his friends I was a virgin and forced me to see *Close Encounters of the Third Kind* three times and listen to nothing but Genesis, which I preferred to The Sex Pistols, because I never believed there was No Future, not when my mother was, at least for now, empty-wombed and full of soul, as she stirred a pot of her famous lentil soup, not yet tied by blood to the man she loved.

Things We Can't Untie

My boyfriend crashed the week before the concert
I'd been waiting for, as if he'd planned to miss it.
I took out Songs of Leonard Cohen, let the record
spin through silence, wiped it clean and put the stylus
where I wanted it, that smooth place in between
the grooves, and waited till it stuck: *I'm not looking*
for another I'm not looking for another I'm not looking
for another I'm not looking for another I'm not looking
for another. I sold my boyfriend's ticket to a girl
with a hunger I could recognise, fought to the front
so Leonard knew my longings, gave me all his songs,
took my tears in return. Later, he signed his name
across my chest and sang *Oh come with me my little one,*
and when he touched my eyes, *our kisses deep*
and warm, and said *We are so small between the stars,*
so large against the sky, I couldn't feel my boyfriend
any more: the leaning green of his Mohican or
The Guns of Brixton lurching through his boom box
that night he took the key of his Triumph Tiger,
scratched it loud across Songs of Leonard Cohen, left me
with a broken record, just because I wouldn't ride
behind him, didn't like to go that fast, because I said
I didn't trust the brakes.

Like a Fish Needs a Bicycle

The first time Jan and Alice came for tea,
they smoked their roll-ups, held hands,
looked purposefully hard. My mother
filled their mugs and smiled a bit too much
before she welcomed them more formally: not
just my little brother's best friend's mothers,
but also *sisters* and *iconoclasts*. Quietly
I sat and braced myself. My mother said

alas she didn't fancy women – no offence
to Jan and Alice – but even so, she longed to
get inside their heads and learn their tricks,
and what exactly did they do in bed and
by the way she totally supported same sex
partnerships or any act of procreation that
involved a turkey baster rather than a man.
Please could they teach her how to be a lesbian?

Both my little brother's new friend's mothers
cleared their throats, but neither spoke. Alice
got up and then sat down again, Jan crunched
on a digestive biscuit. We sipped in unison
in the ensuing silence till at last two roaring boys
charged down the hall stripped to the waist,
wielding makeshift Lego guns, as if they were
the cavalry, to save us from each other.

Sometimes paint spilled and leaked under the door of my stepfather's studio. My mother scrubbed at it with a brillo pad but the stains were ingrained in the carpet. Not many people bought the paintings so we stacked them in rows four-deep against the walls, which made the rooms considerably smaller. Some we fixed to the ceiling just to get them out of the way. If I lay on my back in bed I could see nothing but naked women.

Virginity

Why not get it sorted in that lull
between O Levels and results,
and before I went to Paris
for the summer job
where anything might happen?

I could consider losing it
with Ian who found me fascinating;
ignore his nascent paunch
at only seventeen
forget his parents lived in Borehamwood;

how burdensome,
my mother kept saying, to drag
the weight of it
along with my other baggage
all that way across the English Channel.

The Day My Cousin Took me to the Musée Rodin

Perhaps it was the humid Paris day, perhaps
the naked glory of *Le Baiser* or my blatant boasts
of *l'amour libre* of which I knew, in fact, *rien*
that galvanised my cousin to try his luck with me,

but when he placed one sweaty *main* upon my
firm *nichon* and one upon my *fesse*, I was first
disinclined and then embarrassed. It was clear
he was quite serious, and had in mind, he said,
avec un clin d'œil, a quick and casual act of joy.

When I retorted with grammatical correctness
Je suis ta cousine!, he snorted Frenchly, flushed,
and muttered something vague about *la frigidité
des femmes Anglaises*, tossed his prematurely
balding *tête* and sauntered off into the crowd around

Sculpteur et sa Muse, leaving me *abandonnée* at last
to make some notes, before I took the *métro* home
to find him locked inside his room, his Jewish mother
elbow-deep in worry, onions and gefilte fish.

Volunteers, 1978

The new girls did the bloody work,
chopping the heads off but saving
the necks, yanking out hearts and stomachs
to be boiled for soup. Fat
was managed elsewhere, carcasses removed
and dealt with by superiors.
I went right off chicken.

Good performers were promoted
to onions. I cried all week and chucked
my boyfriend who was on bananas at the time
up a tree from five am till ten
and loving it.

They paid us in airmail letters, cigarettes
and bowls of oranges
and gave us our own bomb shelter
for a disco. I learned
how to smoke, roll a joint and say *I want to
have sex with you,*
in nine different languages.

Sometimes we'd hear them talk;
border skirmishes, patrols around the perimeter,
the occasional funeral.
Someone once told us,
*Keep out of the woods. You might be mistaken
for fedayeen and shot,*
which sounded really, really funny when you were foreign
and nothing to do with it
and stoned.

On Shabbat, there were guests for dinner:
brown, perfect boys fresh
out of school, all big boots and khaki, who'd lope in
smelling of sweat and leather
and lay down their Uzis
like handbags beside steaming bowls
of chicken soup.

Hampstead, 1979

He says he's a Gemini too,
always wears white linen
to parties and is a recreational

heroin user in an open
relationship. He whispers
lunch, writes his number

on a £1 note and yes
on a rainy Friday he buys me
real champagne at Sheekey's,

feeds me oysters with his fingers
pays with the dregs
of his overdraft.

All night he toys with me limply
but lovingly on the floor of
my childhood room

and when The Girlfriend
arrives to pick him up
the next morning as arranged

but two hours early
and his tongue is confusingly in my ear,
it falls to my early-rising mother

to open the door and offer tea
and conversation to The Girlfriend
who admires my mother's

easy way with the I Ching
and spider plants, falls in love with
her collection of African beads

and new alfalfa sprouter and
(my mother tells me later) is slimmer
than I am, with longer hair.

My mother shrank to the size of a small potted plant. The oil paint on the carpet dried into the shape of Africa. She sat in the corner clutching her old skates and dispensing strings of aphorisms on the subject of assertion, the broken record technique and The Swinging Sixties. There were no buttons left on our shirts. Dust lay in drifts on the skirting boards; my mother was too small to keep up with the housework. Needles frightened her.

My Friend Juliet's Icelandic Lover

He floated in through the window
on an ice floe, pissed as a puffin. I sheltered
inside my flannel nightgown
like a Victorian chaperone and trembled
as he exhaled north wind into the room.

While he wrapped you in reindeer furs
you begged me to stay close, whispered
you found him repulsive, smelling
as he did of Brennivin and hákari: you shuddered
at his ghost-white skin, his hairy face.

He was a theatre director from Reykjavik
and you were prim and pretty
with a modest acting talent
and a long term boyfriend who was
perennially unaware.

You were steeped in English waters,
with your permanent pearls and that neat way
you had of sitting with your legs crossed
as if to emphasise what lay
hidden between them

and you listened through the soft
and falling curtain of snow
as he pronounced the reasons why you should.
With him. And why the Fat Friend
who'd never get a man

should go back to her room before
she broke her teeth
with chattering and how you'd never tried a Viking,
had you, Juliet, never heard the word for fuck
in Old Norse –

and still I stayed because you asked me to.
I even forgave you
after I went home to London for a fortnight
because of the pneumonia,
and came back to find you

topless, glowing, perched
on that blue, blue glacier wide enough
to span the narrow hall,
and the flat filled with the smell of him:
putrefied shark, sulphur, crowberry and ice.

Mile End

Not like
the sight of the inedible fish that lay curled
on the plate with its garnish of bright parsley
in that bistro in Curzon Street in 1981 when
you leaned forward to tell me.
More like
when we dropped acid and the branches
were parsley too and the fish heads sang
Don't You Want Me through wet mouths
and your face was a moon, then a sun
and your tongue was on my neck with my
head bent back in the manner of a Chagall.
Not like
when I bought oyster mushrooms in
Petticoat lane as an alibi for my mother
and you told me you'd slept with Jane
and Louise in some room-for-hire in Soho.
Not like
those times you got inside me: once
in the attic at Jocelyn's party, one time
at least after you married Martha who
always said everything was *phenomenal*,
and once after Grace was born.
More like
that other time which reminded me of snow,
but not like
that bistro when, now I come to think of it,
you didn't lean towards me, but away.
More like
that dull Sunday in your hard-to-let flat
in Mile End while Martha was feeding
the baby in the other room and you
murmured *sorry sorry sorry*, one hand
on my cheek, one hand on my hand.

III

The World's Houses

Girls slamming doors mean *I am filled with the loss of myself and the brine of myself and the bursting ridiculous shape of myself and the endless embarrassing spill of myself, and what did I break,*

but boys slamming doors mean only their own reverberant exits in flutters of sawdust, putting hinges out of alignment and shaking floors.

Girls cry from their rooms *Come in, I won't let you in, Come in,*

but boys step out onto streets wearing new, hard hands, those rackety limbs and sprung joints. Someone has taught them to try all the world's houses, someone has told them every door is wide open and theirs for the casual slamming.

Chicken

Knowing no better,
        I had failed to truss the bird
    so its legs and wings were free
to flail on the spit as if it were alive,
        just like the hen my daughter fed and tended
    through that wide and girlish summer,
                the one she volunteered to kill and gut,
    she said, the one she held so gently
        as she tied a loop of string around its neck,
            placed it on the block,
                grasped its feet
                before she swung hard with the axe
            then hung the creature upside down to bleed.
Later, ravenous from harvest work,
        she and the other girls sent a hasty grace
            into the dusk,
        devoured the charred flesh
            and licked clean their small fingers,
soft as the toddler who,
        just yesterday, fell into an enclosure
            at Pittsburgh Zoo
            and was disembowelled
                by a pack of African hunting dogs.
            If you choose to eat an animal,
        you must first learn to kill it,
                my daughter told me
        as I snipped the plastic film,
                plucked some stray feathers
            and rubbed salt into the skin.

My children were pierced and decorated where I was plain. Their evolutionary thumbs grew quick at call and response. I did not know how to compete with their areas of expertise, where or if to place myself on their timelines. I tried not to like their photographs but sometimes I was taken by a terrible mischief.

Mother. Son. Sack of Salt.

It's heavier than it looks.
but she's strong, it's nothing,

and he can help. She takes
one end, he takes the other.

Behind them they leave a trail:
there must be a hole.

Through this walking sleep
that lasts for years, the hands

of the hall clock won't be slowed,
the paintwork peels, the boy

lengthens before her eyes,
the leaking sack grows heavier.

But somewhere on the way
she knows he's taken the weight.

He's strong, he says, it's nothing.
Safe then, for her to let go.

The load is foetus-shaped,
inertly curled against his chest

but he strides forward
and away as if he's carrying

a sack of air, rounds a corner
and he's out of sight.

She hears him take the stairs
lightly, in twos, whistling.

She turns back; follows the trail
of white. She tries to gather up

everything they've left behind,
to fill her arms with salt.

Sometimes home was too close to the edge. The building would fall into the water, or perhaps the water would submerge the building. Either way, it was always a relief to find myself floating downriver towards the barrier where all natural disasters could be prevented.

Leavings

The devils and the lunatics are loose;
bear your children, keep them close

for now. Weave a cocoon of hair and skin,
a silver song to grow them in.

Raise them naked as the angels, sweet
and safe; but mix their milk with grit.

Fold them in love and give them ear and tongue
that they might parley with anyone.

Teach them courage, how to rise and focus.
Muscle them like little boxers.

Wait for it: those fists and minds will soon
turn quicker than your own,

will read this world, will try to cuff or kiss it,
will ask you – *you* – how to fix it.

Shrug; then spin this orb, this creaking prize,
spread out the maps, the changing lines,

throw up your wrinkled hands, unveil the wreck
you've left them: the fires, the slow black,

the cleft and spill. Confess: *this bruised world, blue
and plundered; now it belongs to you.*

When I think of you

I think of dogs and woks and all things green,
onions sweating in the pan, and music,
taste of plenty and the feast of grain,
tofu pressing under heavy bricks,
pot luck suppers, names of vegan beers,
long-abandoned toys in cardboard boxes,
blinks and sighs you think will hide the tears,
of piercings, partings, oceans still to cross,
protests (yours and mine), guitars, tattoos,
my weary age, your optimistic youth,
the way that water soaks through canvas shoes,
of seas that rise to cloud, the common rain,
of continents and shift, roots in the earth,
earth in the blood, of harvest and of change.

– for my son

What time is it in Nova Scotia?

Here, it's 3am, my love, and I can't stop thinking of walruses: historical accounts of sailors who'd trap a calf and torture it until it screamed; the adult animals who heaved their terrible bulk ashore to save their young.

I won't mention nobody's caught the man you ran from but if you come home I swear I'll keep you safe. But I mustn't say come home. Does the heating work? I won't ask about your cough, whether you're eating oranges and learning French or if you like the vest I sent. I wish I could brush your hair. Remind me to send you recipes for soup.

The adult walrus had no predators but man: so many dead, the hunters couldn't take them all and left them piled and useless on the ecoucherie which is French for shore I think but you know that by now if you're learning French.

I won't ask about the terms of your employment, or if you're really healing, or about the lock on your front door and your broken heart, not saying you have a broken heart but if you ever do, that's a lovely, normal thing.

I must go back to sleep, not think about your bicycle, broken locks, dark nights, intruders, walruses. Were they parents too, I wonder, the men who sailed their galleons home laden with carcasses: meat for the voyage, skins for leather, ivory to decorate the wrists of ladies, oil to light the lamps of Europe,

where I am now, oceans away from you at this quiet hour, heavy with the weight of walruses, aching to lay them down, knowing such burdens are not so easily offloaded, the hold of any beast or child, the helpless love one creature must bear another.

On certain occasions, I juggled; or perhaps I threw things. It was hard to tell the difference. Items included my voice, my shoe, myself. Nothing was ever broken although often softened from impact with a wall or floor.

The Melting

We lived with it for days not knowing
what it was
the smell of burning plastic grew familiar
addictive even
but we told ourselves it was the drains
we didn't know the coating on the wires was melting
underneath the floorboards and we might have died
from fumes me and the kids quietly in our beds
if you hadn't come back at last to save us
and tease me
docile like a cow
strange because I knew you fell for me
exactly for my cowness
so I didn't say I'd grown to love the smell
to crave its noxiousness
the tears it siphoned from me and its residue
inside my lungs
I wish you'd listen to me
I never used to wheeze
like this okay yes
I miss its viscous grip
on certain mornings you long gone
and look at my face I'm off again

The Doors to my Daughter's House

I've seen her stride away through meadows
of folding light to the place where the brow of the hill

meets the orchards I planted for her long ago.
I've watched her fill her pack with gold and red.

I've lingered till she's one with the horizon,
willed her towards cities where portals open

like arms, and all the girls are smart and beautiful,
though none so smart and beautiful as she.

She swears she's unpacked the runes, the roses,
the book of edges I composed for her; that she

keeps handy her laugh, her pepper, her third eye,
her delicate cudgel. She's learned to work alone

in the house of many rooms we dreamed up
over nights of moon and milk, the same house

she has made manifest in paper, faith and stone.
Sometimes I knock on the window; sometimes

she lets me in, but quietly, through a dignified gate
in the wall. Blessed with her own sharp glory,

she's made it plain that I must never lean against
those doors she's carved, the ones that swing

open and shut on oiled hinges at intervals
I can't predict, where she stands honed and ready

as the newest weathers of the world rush in and all
her tomorrows poise to make their entrances.

The shop assistant observed that I was shrinking and shivering. She helped me buy a coat to make an extra layer. I felt light and narrow, easy to lift and to carry; my body fluent and well-worked. As a woman greys and hollows this does not mean she should stop working, stop honing, my mother believed. She must recreate desire. Hunger is a good thing. A loosening belt.

IV

Reincarnation

If I could do it over, I think
I'd settle for the zoo variety
of bog-eye, also known as
blue-tongue, shingleback
or stump-tailed skink. I'm tired
of the stink and shape of love,
its naked mating habits, lack
of dignity, all that exposure.
Next time I'll go armoured,
indifferent, put up a token fight
before the quick work of mount
and mate. I'll shrink my heart,
live alone, never look back.
I miss you. I wish I was a skink.

The desk is an heirloom. It's made of imbuia. It belonged to my Lithuanian Grandfather who used it in his consulting room. He died before I was born. There are secret compartments in the back where I hide problematic words in case I need them later. Sometimes they whisper in the dark. At quiet moments, if I put my ear to the ink blotter, I hear the longer ones mount the shorter ones. Weeks or months later, I catch little phrases or cries coming from inside.

Cimex Lectularius

I have learned this week that the common bed bug
can survive for a year without a meal and that Alzheimer's

may be caused by fast food, which reminds me of David Blaine
suspended in a box above the Thames without so much as

a single snack while people pelted him with sausages
and golf balls, how he descended, woozy after 42 days

murmuring *I love you all* as if he had forgotten, which
causes me to wonder at the hunger and delusions of

the loveless, like that anorexic girl in black who jogs
past me every afternoon but never lets me smile at her,

which leads me back intractably to longing and denial.
Perhaps it is something to emulate, the bedbug's stoicism,

how it lives reviled and passive in the cracks, waiting
with quiet certainty for any fool to lie down in the dark.

Kiss/Kiss

Love comes around again, hot pulse in the chest,
so unexpected, so familiar. You pull up a chair
and when we kiss the way we've always kissed

but deeper, all the years of reckoning pressed
between our lips, drifts of old songs in the air,
love comes around again, hot pulse in the chest,

long love, love's work. Who would have guessed
we'd still be here bending time, with time to spare?
And when we kiss the way we've always kissed,

it's like the first kiss. It was raining. I was pissed,
you were surprised; what was it? We didn't care.
Love comes around again, hot pulse in the chest.

Perhaps we knew more wonder then, but now is best:
the old wounds ache and yet we still go there
though when we kiss the way we've always kissed

sometimes it hurts. This kiss comes with a twist:
these wounds we made, each time we kiss them better
love comes around again, hot pulse in the chest.
Let's kiss, my love, again, the way we always kissed.

My father's final wife had hair like my mother's. She was partial to muesli, chunky jewellery and modern art. She bagged up all my old words, took them to the charity shop in her old Honda and redesigned my father's house around him. He was bemused by her jars of lentils, quinoa, stamps, ginseng tea, wholegrain rice, chick peas and rubber bands. He smoked, dozed, shed his hair and occasionally but inadvertently set fire to unfamiliar designer suites.

The Anchor

Sometimes I imagine you dead, and then
I remember open sea from a life before:
that tease of horizon, lovely
inconstant monsters of the deep:
strange, because I love you and the force
of that love is like the drag
of an anchor
tied to a boat
that was once at the mercy of the tides.
This is the chain.
I remember the swift unwinding, each fat link
chafing against the next,
iron claws that burrowed into the sanctuary
of the ocean bed.
Sometimes I dream a sailor's dream:
eternal solitude and water, pregnant stretches of sail,
a salt-skinned sea beneath me, breathing
and pulsing like an animal.

My lover was a celebrated poet who wore sweaters with genuine leather on the elbows. His tomes were hundreds of pages long and not properly edited. One afternoon while he was sleeping I tore out the bad pages and folded them into origami swans. Some floated and some sank, but none of them flew.

Spunk

after Jacob Epstein's *Adam*

His cock hangs at half mast; it's primed to score:
rising, monstrous; nothing like those bland
and flaccid members in rooms 3 and 4.
Drunk on lust, pumped up with blood, he stands
broad on his plinth and howls for cunt. Who'd dare
to leave that call unanswered? This is where
we find the source: that first, primeval sin:
he forced an opening, she let him in.

Later they wrote *she asked for it* – her pink,
seductive flesh, the bruise and not the kiss.
You ask who wrote those books: who do you think?
Would you, with longing, spread your legs for *this*,
bear more like him? It seems so far to fall.
Must this man be the father of us all?

Soup

Jools is the one you go to when
you need a place to cry,
for example, or hot soup, or fashion advice,
Emily says, and while we wait
for the soup we've been craving,
we ask why death, that common leveller, always comes
as a shock, and what if Jools actually dies
on the day Emily's niece gets married; what with
the niece's mother self-medicating
with Seroxat, Surmontil, Benzadrine, unable
to leave the house and the father recovering
from a triple bypass, Emily might have to give the bride
away – ironic considering she can't stand
the groom who always says *pacific* instead of *specific*
and is in recruitment,
so Emily's sleepless with worry and obsessing over
what to buy from the list at John Lewis,
most of it hideous and overpriced, don't I agree,
and she's mortified she's even entertaining
such trivia at a time like this, with Jools on the see-saw
between mindful pain and mindless morphine,
so I in turn confess
I've been wondering what to wear
and would it be inappropriate
to ask Jools to trawl Brick Lane vintage outlets with me
just the way we used to though
she may not live to see the day.
As we pause to gasp at those words that just fell
from my mouth, here's the soup as last;
it's nice, if bland, but we're puzzled
by the texture of the tofu:
spongy with holes. Emily thinks it may be marinated;

67

I say I'm sure my vegan son would know, oh why
               is he living on another continent, and we talk
        about the night he was born:
                    Emily and Jools on their mercy mission
            to the hospital during my long labour bearing
    pizza and ice cubes, the midnight stand-off
            with Nurse Pratt who threatened them with
        forceps and a tube of KY jelly
and suddenly we're in hysterics; me doubled up
    on my wonky wooden chair
            while Emily salts her bowl
                with tears and the waiter stops by to ask
if everything is okay and I want to say there's something wrong
        with the soup; but I tell him
                    yes it's all perfect thank you.

Everlasting

We never kept spares, and one winter's afternoon,
consigned to darkness again, my mother sent me
across the big road for a sixty-watt bayonet bulb,

ten shilling note in my palm, to the hardware shop
where the lady with the beehive hooked one down
from a shelf of shadows, lifted it from its sleeve

and briefly pondered the condition of the filament
before she eased it into the tester, where it blossomed
and held us blinking in its bright circumference.

Sometimes at night, I lie with all my dead beside me
in the absolute dark, and think of that winter, basking
in the longings of the lost who can't be touched again.

But how to let them go: the hardest task is judging
when it's time to flick the switch and let myself
be blinded by the excess radiance of these times,

where, my mother used to say, we had our chance
at the everlasting lightbulb, but in some secret deal,
she claimed, abandoned it.

Since We Last Met

I have narrowed; not as in
diminish, or *dessicate*,
　　　　more as in *sliver*, *float*
　　　　　　　and *stop-out-late*.
If you were to embrace me,
　　　　　as in *dread* or *long-for*
you would find me less of a daughter,
　　　　not as in *shrink* or *predicate*,
more as a *slip-between-grooves*,
　　rise and *sinuous-of-spine*.
If I were to speak myself,
　　　not as in *whine* or *small talk*
　　　　but as in *create*:
you would see me as a fine line,
　　　　as in *tapered*, *weightless*,
　　　　　　that loops itself
　　under reading lights
　　　　as in *inked* and *driven*,
in a neighbourhood you loved to hate
and scorned to visit
but always dreamed you lived in.

Late at night my mother could be found seated at the kitchen table dispensing lentil soup, judgements, charms and home truths. Fat friends were exhorted to live on eggs, solitary ones to frequent art galleries and public parks, nervous ones to stand on their heads, plain ones to wear hats. My mother collected their tears in her ladle and used them to season the soup.

Valentine For Turbulent Times

When you open your eyes to find great love
beside you and you tease open the heart
with kisses and coffee and you yawn and yearn
and reach towards this snowdrop morning,
a few lines of bliss might achieve lift-off
but for the cacophonous news that rolls
across your horizon grinning from
its armoured tank as it exits the hatch
to trip you up with its big dirty boots, even
before you have a chance to rise. And love?
There it is, running from fire and terror,
small and useless like the unseasonal
ladybird crawling across this page,
confused about what to do with its wings.

Charm for Late Love

Here we go again, my old crow.
I'll ride your boneback, edge and turn,
up where the windsongs coil and glow,
feathers fall and currents churn.
Candle Gutter Flare and Burn

Let the stars drip sodden light.
We'll find the shine once more, we'll name
our quarry, rattle it through night:
let's taste the blood of the ancient game.
Candle Snuff Gutter and Flame

Let's wing it, old crow, deny the laws
of chance. How hard it is to catch
and hold a joy in yellowed claws,
to risk the slip, outface the crash.
Candle Gutter Snuff and Ash

Let your straitened wings unfold,
eclipse the moon with a surge and sweep
through grip and glint of marrowcold.
Let's hunt the heart we'll never keep.
Candle Gutter Snuff and Sleep

Acknowledgements

Many thanks to the editors of the following publications in which some of these poems first appeared, sometimes in previous versions:

Poetry Review, The Rialto, Ambit, Magma Poetry, The Emma Press Anthology of Motherhood, The Jewish Quarterly, Writing Motherhood Blog, Under the Radar, Double Bill (Red Squirrel Press), *Binders Full of Women, The Morning Star, POEM magazine.* Some of the prose poems appeared in *If I Lay on my Back I Saw Nothing but Naked Women,* published by The Emma Press in 2014. *My Friend Juliet's Icelandic Lover* won Second prize in the Ledbury Poetry Competition, *The Anchor* won second prize in the Essex Poetry Competition, *Chicken* was commended in the Ware Poetry Competition and *Cimex Lectularius* was longlisted in the National Poetry Competition.

With immeasurable thanks to my dear friends Norbert Hirschhorn, Anja König, Rosie Shepperd and Clare Pollard who read and commented on many of these poems individually and provided thoughts on the manuscript in development. Gratitude to Stephen Knight, Philip Gross, Ron Carey and Helen Beetham for all their support and insights on the collection as it grew. Thank you to Jane Commane for her faith in these poems and her inspired editing. Thank you to my daughters and sons for endless cups of tea and encouragement at difficult moments. Love and thanks as always to Robin for everything, all of it.